Lead a life of

CONFIDENCE

Free yourself of fear, anxiety and frustration

Dale Furtwengler

FAI Publications
St. Louis, MO

Cover illustration by Nicole Cooper
St. Louis, MO

This publication is designed to provide accurate and authoritative information to the subject matter covered. It is sold with the understanding that the publisher is not engaged in rendering legal, accounting, or other professional advice. If legal advice or other expert assistance is required, the services of a competent professional person should be sought.

Furtwengler, Dale.
    Lead a life of confidence : free yourself of fear, anxiety and frustration/ by Dale Furtwengler.

ISBN-13: 978-0692364703
ISBN-10: 0692364706

1. Confidence. 2. Fear. 3. Anxiety. 4. Frustration. I. Title

Cover illustration by Nicole Cooper, St. Louis, MO

TABLE OF CONTENTS

I want your life!   1

1   Not if ..., but how much?   3
        Spectral confidence   *3*
        Situational confidence   *5*

2   Defining success   9
        Dealing with others   *9*
        Opportunities   *10*
        The role of success   *11*

3   The language of success   14

4   Talent, success and happiness   16

5   Not what you know, it's...   19

6   Competing...with whom?   23

7   When your best falls short   27

8   One is the loneliest number   29
        Family and friends   *29*
        Other people's experiences *30*
        Finding support   *31*

9   Other people's perceptions   34

10   The cardinal rule of goals   37

11   An overnight success?   40

12   Recovery shots   43

13   Virtually free   45

14   Conscious vs. subconscious?   48

15   Contentment vs. desire?   52
     Contentment   *52*
     Desire   *53*

16   Accelerating growth   55

17   Expressing confidence   57
     Calm   *57*
     Candid   *60*
     Caring   *61*

18   Living with confidence   63
     Desire   *64*
     Expectations   *64*
     Aware   *69*
     Deliberate   *70*
     Influential   *71*
     Joyful   *72*

Daily Confidence Builder   74

About the Author   78

It is one of the most beautiful compensations in life...that no man can sincerely try to help another without helping himself.

— Ralph Waldo Emerson

I want your life!

Never, in my wildest dreams, did I expect to hear these words directed to me. Yet, in the past three years, more than a half-dozen people have told me that they want my life.

When I challenge their declaration, they say:

- I want to do what I want, when I want, like you do.
- I want to avail myself of opportunities without worrying about the consequences the way you do.
- I want to take time off to travel like you do.

What they're really saying is that they want to be free of fear, anxiety and frustration, something I hadn't realized I had achieved. This realization begged the question "What is it that enables me to lead a virtually worry-free existence?"

The short answer is confidence. But that raised another question "How had I gained that confidence?" It didn't exist early in my life. In fact, despite growing up in one of the most encouraging, nurturing environments anyone could hope to have, I was a shy, insecure child. I feared meeting people because I didn't know what to say to them.

Over time, with self-help reading and an Ann Landers' insight, I became a person who initiates conversations in elevators. During my transition from shy child to gregarious adult, I learned a lot about confidence. I learned that much of the fear, anxiety and frustration people experience is the by-product of their:

- Definition of success.
- Ill-defined goals.
- Unrealistic expectations.
- Blind acceptance of other people's perceptions.

Whenever I share these discoveries with others, they urge me to put them into writing so that more people can enjoy a worry-free existence. *Lead a Life of CONFIDENCE* is written to honor their wish and mine that you enjoy a life virtually free of fear, anxiety and frustration.

— Dale Furtwengler

CHAPTER 1
Not if..., but how much?

When we speak of confidence, we say "She's confident" or "He lacks confidence." Implicit in this language is the presumption that confidence is binary—that a person has it or doesn't. The reality is that confidence is both spectral and situational.

Spectral

Each of us possesses confidence in some areas of our lives. What varies from person to person is the frequency and intensity with which we express that confidence. The following Likert scale gives you a way to measure the frequency with which you express confidence *in any given area of your life*.

CONFIDENT				
Rarely	Occasionally	Usually	Frequently	Consistently

Viewing confidence as a spectrum opens the door to all sorts of possibilities for you.

Once you realize that you are confident in some areas of your life, you can tap into that confidence to gain greater confidence in other areas. Later in the book, you'll discover how to do that.

In the meantime, we're going to explore an element of human nature that often prevents us from ranking higher on the confidence spectrum.

One of the fascinating, and often debilitating, aspects of human nature is that we tend to focus on the negative. The memories of our failings are more vivid than those of our successes. To understand why, let's explore how our minds process success and failure.

Success

Many of us think our successes are nothing special, nothing extraordinary. The reason is that these successes come so naturally that we mistakenly believe that they have little value. Nothing could be further from the truth. The things you're able to accomplish in a few minutes may take me hours to achieve, if I can achieve them at all. Yet you discount your success because it comes easily.

Success that comes naturally doesn't seem special; consequently, it generates little, if any, memory. Your mind naturally filters out the mundane to allow quicker access to what's important to you. That's the reason why everyday successes don't trigger lasting memories. Unfortunately, that isn't true for failures.

Failure

Failures are painful and pain triggers vivid memories. That's a safety mechanism our minds have developed. It's the reason why only one experience of touching something scorchingly hot reminds us not to do it again.

Unfortunately, this safety mechanism can't distinguish between physical pain and emotional pain. Consequently, the emotional pain associated with failure is every bit as vivid as memories of physical pain. Because memories of failures are so vivid, they come to mind more readily than memories of our successes. It's this aspect of our humanity that explains why it's so easy to lose confidence.

The more frequently you recall failures, the more hits your self-confidence takes, the greater the likelihood you'll be trapped into a life of fear, anxiety and frustration. Fortunately, it doesn't have to be that way.

Altering memories

You have the capability to make memories of your success more vivid while diminishing memories of your shortcomings. In chapter 2, Defining Success, you'll discover the secret to making success more memorable. It's a simple process that not only increases the confidence you possess, but enables you to extend that confidence into areas of your life in which it didn't previously exist. Before we move to chapter 2, let's explore the situational nature of confidence.

Situational

Just as confidence manifests in varying degrees of frequency and intensity, it also varies from situation to situation. In my youth, I felt wholly inadequate when meeting new people; I didn't know what to say to them.

In sports, my confidence was a little higher. I didn't hesitate to try out for teams even though I knew others were more talented. But when it came to school work, I was supremely confident.

Confidence in my ability to learn not only enabled me to excel in school, it fueled my transformation from shy, insecure child to gregarious adult. That's the kind of impact you can expect as you discover your confidence.

Your confidence varies from situation to situation. Let's figure out where your confidence lies and to what degree it exists. To help you with this analysis, take a sheet of paper and draw a vertical line down the center.

Don't overthink this exercise, go with what first comes to mind. On the left side list five things you really enjoy doing; on the right, list a similar number of things you dread doing.

Rank the items you enjoy in descending order (most enjoyable to least enjoyable). Do the same with the items you dread (greatest dread to least dread). You've identified the degree of confidence you possess in each of these situations. Now let's put that knowledge to work for you.

Confidence resides in joy; things you enjoy doing are the ones you do well. The opposite is true for things you dread. One of the reasons you dread these tasks is that you struggle while performing them. The more you struggle, the greater the hit to your confidence.

There may be things you feel confident doing, but don't enjoy. Some may even be on your list, but the bulk of your list will indicate where your confidence lies and where it's lacking.

This knowledge is essential because, as you remind yourself of situations in which you are confident, you can tap that confidence to help you deal with situations in which you're less confident. That presumes that you want to gain confidence in these areas.

Desire

It's okay to forgo confidence in situations you intend to avoid. I'm not comfortable with heights. If rock climbing, sky diving, or bungee jumping were intriguing to me, I'm confident I'd overcome my fear. Because they aren't, I choose to hire people to handle roof and gutter repairs. Outsourcing these tasks allows me to devote my time and energy to building confidence in areas that do appeal to me.

I am confident that I'd overcome my fear of heights because I overcame my fear of meeting new people. I also overcame my fear of the water to become a certified scuba diver. I've discovered the tools and techniques needed to conquer fear.

That knowledge, when coupled with a *desire* to do something that intrigues me, provides the confidence I need to be successful. The only difference between the situations described above is that I *desire* the joy of other people's company and scuba diving, I don't have a desire to climb mountains, sky dive or bungee jump.

When you understand this distinction, and train your mind to make conscious choices, you'll no longer view yourself as someone who lacks confidence. Instead, you'll be confident in the knowledge that you can overcome your fear *if* what you desire is truly important to you.

Instead of experiencing fear and anxiety, you'll take comfort in knowing that you can overcome your fear, if it's important to you to do so. That's a huge difference.

As you can see, the question isn't whether you're confident —it's *not if* you're confident, but *how much* confidence you possess, where it resides and *how much* of it you express.

When you realize you're confident, you can use this knowledge to move your confidence from its current position on the Likert scale to "consistently" for all areas of your life.

As confidence grows you'll experience greater joy and success, which brings us to chapter 2's topic—how your definition of success impacts confidence.

CHAPTER 2
Defining success

Even the most confident among us experience fear, anxiety and frustration. It's part of the human condition. The difference between the most and least confident is the speed with which they're able to set aside doubts and fears. That ability hinges on their definition of success.

While transitioning from shy, insecure child to gregarious adult, I discovered the secret to success *regardless of the outcome*. On the surface that seems an inane if not insane statement, but here's what I learned.

Dealing with others

The key to success when dealing with others is to craft several options, any of which are acceptable to you (including the option for the other person to say "No"), then allow the other person to choose. Regardless of their choice you get what you want. The outcome is a success.

If the other person chooses any option other than "No," you get what you desire. If you get a "No," you avoid wasting time and energy pursuing an outcome that isn't viable. That's why, regardless of what the other person chooses, you'll enjoy a successful outcome.

A similar insight emerged for new opportunities.

Opportunities

New opportunities are a mixed blessing; while they're intriguing and exciting, they also generate fear and doubt.

Opportunities beg questions like:

- Is this something I really want?
- What if I later discover that it's not what I want?
- Can I survive a bad choice financially?
- How will my decision impact my family?
- Do I have the skills and experience to be successful?
- How long will it take to find another opportunity if this doesn't work?

That's a lot of fear and anxiety.

Over the years I've been blessed with many opportunities, here's what I learned. If I embraced the opportunity and it worked, I was successful. If it didn't, but I learned something, the venture was still a success.

At one point in my career I couldn't find the kind of job I was seeking, so I attempted a commission sales job. "Attempted" is an accurate description. I had the third-highest gross in the office and wondered what everyone else was living on—I wasn't making that much money. Eight months later I found employment better suited to my skills.

Many people would consider that experience a failure. For me, it was a huge success—one that I treasure to this day. The discovery I made laid the foundation for a much brighter future for me and my family.

I learned that I have difficulty selling things over which I have little control. This awareness proved invaluable years later when I established my consulting business. I was confident in my ability to sell *my* consulting services because I controlled the process.

I'm also adept at avoiding situations in which I know I can't be successful—whether it's because I lack skills or experience, because I don't enjoy the work, or because I doubt the client will do his part.

The knowledge I gained from that commission sales job helped me enjoy levels of income in my consulting business that more than offset any income I had forgone during my eight months in that job.

Now that we've defined success, let's explore its psychological impact on confidence.

The role of success

Confidence expands and contracts based upon your perceptions of success and failure. Perceived failures diminish your confidence. When you feel that you've failed, every encounter with other people triggers the fear that your inadequacies are obvious—that you have "failure" imprinted on your forehead.

You perceive others as being more successful and, hence, more worthy of future success. You wonder "Why would this person want to associate with me?" Your doubts and fears become negative vibes that repel rather than attract others. The more others avoid your negative vibes, the more your fears are affirmed—others don't want to associate with you—and your confidence wanes.

When your memories are replete with your latest failing, you're more likely to walk away from new opportunities. You don't want to experience the sympathetic looks of family and friends should you fail again. Nor do you want to suffer "I told you so" from naysayers in your life.

You avoid financial risk. You're concern about the welfare of your family, and the financial burden another failure would place on them, precludes you from seeing the potential of a more financially-secure future for them. It doesn't have to be that way.

Using your new definitions of success, you're assured success in every human interaction and every opportunity. When someone says "no" to your offer, that person saves you a lot of time and energy,

freeing you to pursue others who may have an interest in what you offer. Ask any successful salesperson and they'll tell you that it isn't the "No" that carries the heaviest cost, it's the "Maybe."

Similarly, when you avail yourself of an opportunity and the result is disappointing, it's still a success *if you learn something*. In classes I teach I tell students that if they make a mistake and learn something, its an investment. It's when they don't learn anything from the experience that it's an expense. I've made more than my fair share of mistakes over the years, but I made sure that they were investments—investments that paid huge dividends in my life.

Avail yourself of new opportunities confident in the knowledge that, at the very least, you're going to learn something about yourself that will benefit you in years to come. Never again fret over getting a "No" when you know that it's going to save you time and energy that you can devote to more profitable pursuits.

When success is assured, there's nothing to prevent you from pursuing what you desire. With each success your confidence grows and extends to other areas of your life. You'll find yourself moving closer to the "consistently" end of the confidence spectrum *because you've discovered the definition of success.*

Now that you have a definition of success, let's see how the language you use impacts the success you enjoy.

CHAPTER 3
The language of success

Frustrated with repeated attempts to lose weight, I told a friend that I'd decided to get healthy—to exercise more and let my weight find its natural level.

"You will be successful this time" he said. I asked how he could be so certain. He responded "Because you're goal is to gain health, not lose weight."

He explained that the reason weight-loss programs fail is that the goal is to lose weight. He asked "What do you want to do when you lose something?"

"I want to get it back, but I don't want the weight back once I've lost it."

"Of course not, but you want your old lifestyle back."

I had never thought of weight loss in this way; yet what he said made perfect sense. His prediction came true—my new goal yielded better health and sustained weight loss.

My friend later explained that he is a neuro-linguistic programming (NLP) practitioner. NLP is the study of the impact language has on behavior. The more I read on the topic, the more I could see how powerful language is in determining success or the lack thereof.

The language of gain nurtures success, whereas the language of fear, anxiety and loss fosters disappointment.

14

Some of you may be wondering "How is NLP different than the law of attraction?" The core concepts are similar. They both link a positive mindset to favorable outcomes and negative mindset to disappointment.

The law of attraction suggests that when you envision yourself enjoying what you desire, you attract it. NLP uses language to effect the behavioral changes necessary to acquire what you desire. This may seem like a subtle difference, but I can tell you that, after trying both, NLP works much better for me.

In my opinion, the law of attraction has the potential to mislead people into thinking that envisioning (wishing) is enough to get what they desire. That hasn't been my experience; I've had to make NLP-induced behavioral changes to achieve my goals.

The next time you find yourself struggling to achieve your goal, take a look at the language used in establishing it. Is it the language of gain? Or is it the language of scarcity, avoidance or prevention? If it's the latter, change your language and develop a new action plan to gain what you truly desire.

Now that you have a sense for the role language plays in your success, let's explore the role of talent.

CHAPTER 4
Talent, success and happiness

We often equate success, talent and happiness. While there may be some correlation, it's not significant. How can I be so emphatic? Whenever I explore a topic, I look first to the incongruities between the premise proffered and what I'm observing.

In this instance, the presumption is that there's a high correlation between talent, success, and happiness. Is this true? Not according to my observations.

We need look no farther than celebrities' lives to gain visible evidence that talent and success do not assure happiness. Having said that, there are examples of incredibly talented people who've enjoyed tremendous success and great happiness—Michael Jordan, Arnold Palmer, Morgan Freeman, Reba McEntire come readily to mind. Unfortunately, there's a flip side to that coin.

We've also seen inordinately talented celebrities who've enjoyed great professional success, but were plagued with doubts, fears and frustrations. Michael Jackson, Robin Williams and Philip Seymour Hoffman, after experiencing years of psychological pain, met tragic ends.

16

These observations indicate that while talent and success may contribute to happiness, they don't assure it. Why is this important? It eliminates lack of talent as a reason for your lack of success.

Don't blame your lack of success on a lack of talent. It's more likely that it's your definition of success, the language you use to establish goals, or a lack of desire on your part that are to blame.

The reality is that each of us possesses talents. I've been told that my talents lie in my ability to:

- Find simple solutions to complex problems.
- Communicate succinctly.
- Understand human nature.

That's a tiny set of talents when measured against all the talent that exists in this world. Yet despite my limited talent pool, people express a desire to have my life. That's what I want for you.

I want you to acknowledge and appreciate the talent you possess while being comfortable in the knowledge that no one comes with the complete package. I can't imagine a more boring existence than one in which I knew everything—had nothing new to learn.

It's the pursuit of knowledge and personal bests that makes life exciting. That's true regardless of the level of talent you possess or where that talent resides.

As an adjunct professor at the University of Missouri-St. Louis, I regularly see students who don't possess the IQ of their more gifted colleagues, outperform those same colleagues.

A dog trainer in St. Louis established a very successful school to teach others to become dog trainers when he realized that he was winning competitions with less-talented dogs.

This isn't news to you. You know people who possess incredible talent, but aren't doing much with that talent. You also know less-talented people who excel at whatever they choose to do. Hard work and perseverance drive their success. It's not the talent that matters, it's what we do with it.

The legendary Green Bay Packers' coach, Vince Lombardi, said "The measure of who we are is what we do with what we have."

His statement acknowledges that there will always be someone who possesses more talent than we do and that no one comes with the complete package.

There's also an awareness that a lack of talent need not prevent you from enjoying great success or incredible happiness. You have a right to both. The key is making the most of whatever talent you possess in the pursuit of what you desire.

Confidence isn't a function of talent, but what you do with that talent. In a similar vein, confidence isn't based on what you know, but in... You'll find out in chapter 5.

CHAPTER 5
Not what you know, it's...

It saddens me to see bright, talented, hardworking people forgo opportunities because they don't feel they have the experience they need to be successful. When I ask them why they're passing up a great opportunity, they say "I don't know how to..." or "I don't have experience with..."

If knowledge and experience were prerequisites for success, how could we explore space, develop nanotechnologies or devise surgical instruments and techniques employed today? Advancements aren't driven by what's known, they're driven by the confidence people have in their ability to learn and adapt.

Take a moment and imagine a world in which experience and knowledge are required for advancement. What does it look like? We need only go back a few centuries to get a glimpse of that world.

In those days if you were cobbler's son, you became a cobbler. You learned your father's trade and passed your knowledge onto your sons. Women were homemakers and guardians of their children's welfare. That's the knowledge they passed onto their daughters.

Under these conditions, the world remains static. We might see incremental progress, but few major advancements. The reason is that new ideas would be dismissed on the basis that there was no experience or knowledge to support their viability. It's not what you know that matters, but your ability to learn and adapt.

I have two vivid memories that highlight this fact. The first was forty years ago when I was with a national CPA firm. I was given an assignment to assist a client that had been the subject of a wage and hour audit. I protested the assignment on the basis that I didn't have any wage and hour experience. Fortunately my protest was ignored.

I thought the assignment was to make sure that the client wasn't being overcharged for back wages and penalties. An hour into the project, the client's top executive asked "Dale, what are you doing?"

"Making sure that you're not being overcharged."

To which he responded, "You don't understand, we want to fight these charges." Gulp.

I got a copy of the charges and began interviewing managers and staff. I quickly discerned that the charges were baseless. I drafted a letter challenging the audit findings, had it reviewed by the partner-in-charge, then forwarded the letter to the client's CEO for signature. A couple of months later, all charges were dropped.

If I had to rely on my knowledge of wage and hour law or prior experience in that field, we'd have been doomed. It was my ability to learn what I needed to know along with my ability to adapt what I'd learned in other aspects of my life, that enabled me to produce a successful outcome for our client.

The second memory that affirms this truth came years later. I'd completed my second interview for a new job and we had agreed on terms of employment.

As I stood to leave, one of the principals said "By the way, Dale, you'll be responsible for credit and collection as well. Is that okay?" "Of course!" I responded. As I walked out the door I thought "I've got to get to the library, I know nothing about credit and collection."

My confidence in my ability to learn enabled me to accept these additional responsibilities. If prior knowledge or experience were a prerequisite, I'd have had to turn down this opportunity. I can't help but wonder how many of you have forgone opportunities because of a lack of experience or knowledge. That never has to happen again. Your ability to learn is the only tool you need to avail yourself of new opportunities.

I'm not unique in my ability to learn. Think of the things you've learned over the years—things in which you had no prior experience or knowledge. Your first teetering steps exemplified a belief, albeit a subconscious belief, in your ability to walk. You had no facility for language, yet today you're able to read, write and speak. You've learned about science, math, grammar, and an astounding array of other subjects.

Certainly some things are easier to learn than others, that's true for all of us. Having said that, I'll bet that the struggles you've had learning have more to do with your interest level than you're ability to learn.

When you realize that you're ability to succeed comes from your ability to learn, adapt and refine, not from what you know, you'll avail yourself of more opportunities. In the process, you'll develop new abilities, gain additional confidence and experience greater joy in every aspect of your life.

In chapters 4 and 5 we acknowledged that there are people who possess more talent than we do and who know more than we do. That awareness begs the question "How do we compete with these people?" You'll discover the answer to that question in chapter 6.

CHAPTER 6
Competing...with whom?

Attitudes toward competition are changing. For my generation competing is a way of life. You pit your skills against others' skills and the winner took the prize. You competed for a spot on the team, grades, entry into the best colleges, scholarships, jobs, a mate and a better life for your family. If you won, great! If you lost, you'd look for ways to win the next time.

Today, a growing number of people believe that competition is unhealthy, particularly for kids. They feel that competition is not only stressful, it can adversely affect a child's confidence. In what has historically been competitive events, they advocate giving every child a medal or trophy demonstrating that there are no losers.

Implicit in both attitudes is the presumption that everyone deals with competition in precisely the same way. A presumption you know isn't true. You know people who live to be tested—who thrive in highly-competitive environments. The greater the challenge, the happier they are.

Others dread competition; some even find it debilitating. These people often collapse under pressure, fail miserably, and take serious hits to their confidence.

The vast majority of us adopt the old adage "you win some, you lose some." It's the way life works. The reality is that competition's impact on confidence depends, like success, upon its definition. I learned this from one of my clients.

This client encouraged competition while promoting growth in confidence. Above the entryway my client displayed a board that celebrated all team members who had achieved a new *personal* best.

This system recognizes that while talent and skills vary from individual to individual, the real measure of success is how much you've improved over your previous best. In others words, the only legitimate competition is with yourself.

Pro golfers seem to be more well attuned to this attitude than most competitors. When questioned about their performance, they compare that day's outing to their prior outings, not other players' performance. Pro golfers realize that the only thing they can control is their own performance.

They can't control weather or course conditions, which change as the day progresses. They have no control over the fact that some players get hot, while others lose their touch. None of these things are under the pro golfer's control. The only thing that professional golfers can control is their performance.

The late Ken Venturi, pro golfer and broadcaster, described golf as a game of getting it, losing it and getting it back again. Sounds a lot like life doesn't it?

I'm not suggesting that competition against others is unhealthy. You can learn a great deal about yourself and how to improve by competing against people more talented, experienced, and successful than you are. Here's an example to illustrate my point.

In the early years of my consulting business, I served as program chair for a consultants' association. Somehow I had the good sense to populate the program committee with seasoned consultants.

During our first planning meeting they began discussing books and concepts that were completely foreign to me. I realized that I had been deluding myself about how well prepared I was to help my clients. They were more aggressive and eclectic learners than I was.

That meeting became the driving force for me to elevate my game, which enhanced my success as well as that of my clients. That wouldn't have been possible if I hadn't seen what my "competitors" had achieved.

It's even worthwhile to compete when you *know* you're going to lose. When my brother and I were much younger, he was really into tennis. He joined a club, participated in ladder events, had himself taped and coached by pros to improve his game.

I was the complete opposite. I was a recreational player. I played two or three times a month and *never* practiced.

When my brother and I got together to play, I knew I was going to lose. I also played some of the best tennis I ever played. I learned a lot from those losses and enjoyed every minute of it. Why wouldn't I? I learned something.

The keys to using competition to grow your confidence are:

• Acknowledging that there will always be someone better than you—more talented, more skilled or more experienced.

- Understanding that competing against those better than you helps you elevate your game and enriches your future.
- Recognizing that, at the end of the day, the only person you're really competing against is yourself.

These realizations, when combined with your new definition of success, assure that you'll always be a winner. The more often you win, the more confident you become.

In this chapter we've discussed what happens to your confidence when you achieve a new personal best. But what happens when you best falls short? That's the question we'll answer in chapter 7.

CHAPTER 7
When your best falls short

As a professional speaker I take no pride in telling you that I've had days when I couldn't string two fluid sentences together if my life depended on it. I'm sure you've had days like that. No matter what you do, how hard you try or how long you persevere, your results are disappointing.

I recall a day near the end of my second year in business when I realized that my revenues for the month were almost as bad as they were in my very first month in business. I told my wife, "I've got to be nuts. I tell people that I can help them improve their bottom line and I can't even generate decent revenues for myself."

Who among us hasn't experienced similar frustrations? These experiences threaten our confidence. But should they?

My youngest brother answers this way, "I've never met a person whose graph is a straight line up and to the right." He completes his thought saying "I've never met a player who, at some point, hasn't made a lateral move or taken a step back to get ahead."

In other words, each of us experiences plateaus and occasional declines in performance. The question is "How do you maintain your confidence in the face of adversity so that you can persevere while pursuing your new personal best?"

One of the best answers I've found came from a book entitled *The Four Agreements* by Don Miguel Ruiz. Here's what he says:

"Under any circumstance, always do your best, no more and no less. But keep in mind that your best is never going to be the same from one moment to the next. Everything in life is changing all the time, so your best will sometimes be high quality, and other times it will not be as good."

As soon as I read that passage my mind traveled back to those days as a speaker when things didn't go well. I recalled that, despite a poor performance, there were people who came up and said "This is the message I needed to hear today. Thank you."

These moments reminded me that the quality of my delivery is secondary to the quality of the message. As long as I provide useful information, the audience forgives a less than stellar performance *if* they sense that I'm trying to do my best.

Thanks to Mr. Ruiz I gained comfort in the knowledge that I did my best on those days and my messages added value even though I struggled. His encouraging words enable me to continue my pursuit of new personal bests confident in the knowledge that I'll achieve them—someday.

You may be thinking "I can cope with the occasional bad day, but how do I remain confident when months or years go by without any progress?" The next three chapters are dedicated to answering this question.

CHAPTER 8
One is the loneliest number

Those of you from my generation probably recognize the title of this chapter; it's gleaned from a Three Dog Night song. This title bespeaks the irrefutable fact that none of us accomplishes anything on our own.

I've had many teachers, academic and non-academic, who have contributed mightily to my success. Their lessons are as vivid today as the day I learned them. Their wisdom, and generosity in sharing that wisdom, enable me to enjoy a life others desire. But they aren't the only contributors.

Family and friends

In the previous chapter I shared my frustration that during my second year in business I experienced revenues as paltry as my first month in business. You recall the rant in which I said to my wife "I've got to be nuts. I tell people that I can help them improve their bottom line and I can't even generate decent revenues for myself."

She calmly responded "Dale, it's one month. Look at the trend, the trend is good. You can't let one month derail you."

What struck me most about her statement is that her need for financial security is much greater than mine. Yet she encouraged me to stay the course. Her words were exactly what I needed to lift myself out of self-pity and get back to work.

My wife's observation was accurate. A few months later revenues accelerated so quickly that it felt as if the business had gained a life of its own—a momentum that couldn't be stopped.

Of course there've been times during the past 25 years when, as my brother says, the graph wasn't a straight line up and to the right. Yet I weathered them easily thanks to my wife's encouraging words.

Other people's experiences

Daymond John, co-founder of fashion empire, FUBU, and shark on *Shark Tank*, says "There are many people who will help you in regard to your success, but you are the only one responsible for your failures."

The success I've enjoyed rests squarely on the lessons and encouragement I've received from others. It's unlikely that I'd have written this book if friends and colleagues hadn't insisted that others would benefit from these messages.

At the same time, my "failures" are of my own doing. I placed the word "failures" in quotes because it's not in my vocabulary. This word violates the definitions of success as well as the NLP concept of gain, and, in the process, threatens confidence.

What many people consider to be failures are really altered choices. If, while pursuing a goal, you discover that the goal isn't important enough for you to continue its pursuit and you choose to abandon its pursuit, that's not a failure. It's an altered choice.

My interest in scuba diving enabled me to overcome my fear of the water to become a certified diver. I have no interest in rock climbing, sky diving or bungee jumping, consequently, I have no desire to overcome my fear of heights. Does that make me a failure? I don't think so. Overcoming my fear of heights is not a priority in my life. Nor should it be.

There are many other things I aspire to achieve. Some of them will require me to overcome fears and doubts I have. My time and energy should be devoted to overcoming these obstacles.

Finding support

You need people who'll remind you of your success, help you redefine failure, support you during your darkest hours. There will be dark hours—hours during which you'll wonder, as I did, whether you're nuts to think you can accomplish your goal.

That's when you need people in your corner who not only believe in you, but look for ways to help you realize your dreams. Not all of us are fortunate enough to have family members to fill that role, sometimes friends are our greatest advocates. You can't choose your family, but you can choose your friends.

In a television interview, tennis champions Venus and Serena Williams stated that sometimes you have to leave long-time friends behind and develop new friends. They said that when they shared their dream of being elite tennis champions with childhood friends, their friends said that they were crazy.

The Williams sisters realized that their friends weren't dreaming as big as they were, that they needed friends who would encourage rather than dissuade them. They needed people who'd help them get through periods of self-doubt, fear and anxiety. They realized that they couldn't get that from people who didn't believe in them, who didn't dream as big as they did. Nor can you.

The Williams sisters said that it was hard to leave childhood friends. They are good people; but they weren't the people to help the sisters realize their dreams. Venus and Serena made the difficult, conscious decision to leave long-time friends and make new ones. They attribute much of their success to the encouragement and confidence bestowed upon them by their new friends.

How important is your dream to you? Is it important enough to leave long-time friends for more supportive friends? Regardless of your answer, you need to make a *conscious* decision. I emphasize the word conscious because, if you don't make a conscious decision, you may experience guilt, fear and obligation.

Guilt for having slighted friends, the fear of losing them and an obligation to them because they helped you weather previous storms.

A conscious decision enables you to acknowledge, to them and yourself, the gratitude you feel for their friendship and support while honoring your dream. If they're good friends, they'll respect your candor and wish you the best.

None of us accomplishes anything alone. We need the wisdom, encouragement and support of others to achieve our goals. If these people don't exist in your life, find them and develop mutually-supportive friendships. Choose your friends wisely and consciously. They're the ones who'll help you persevere during the months and years it takes to achieve your goal, including the dark hours.

While we need others to help us achieve our goals, it pays to be cautious when evaluating their input as you'll discover in chapter 9.

CHAPTER 9
Other people's perceptions

We can learn a great deal about ourselves from other people, but we can also be mislead by their perceptions. Here are some personal experiences to illustrate this point.

I joined our basketball team in elementary school. My dad knew the coach. One day, in a casual conversation, the coach told my dad that I'd play more if I were more aggressive. When my dad relayed this message, I thought "I'm just playing by the rules."

Despite my belief, I embraced the coach's assessment. I accepted the perception that I wasn't aggressive. I even considered the possibility that I was apathetic. I held this self-image for nearly twenty years.

It changed as I was leaving my first controllership position. I was about to walk out the door when the head bookkeeper told me that the owner, *on the day he hired me*, told her not to get used to having me around. He said I was too aggressive; that he wouldn't be able to keep me for long.

I was astounded. For decades I lived with the assumption that I wasn't aggressive. I couldn't help wonder "Was I wrong all those years? Was I more aggressive than I realized? Was my aggression only related to career pursuits, not physical activities? Which perception of my nature was accurate?"

As I explored these questions, I realized that, like everyone else, I'm aggressive in pursuing things I desire; less so in pursuing things of little importance to me.

The dichotomy of these two perceptions of my nature helped me understand that aggressiveness, like confidence, isn't a question of whether it exists—it exists. What varies among individuals is the intensity and frequency with which it's expressed and the situations in which it's expressed.

I enjoyed playing basketball, but didn't have a desire to excel at it. Had I been more interested I have no doubt that I would have devoted more time and energy to understanding my strengths and, possibly, have been more aggressive in employing them.

How can my experiences help you? Here's what I've learned. I appreciate the perceptions others share with me regarding my nature, strengths and weaknesses, however, I no longer accept them at face value. Instead, I ask myself:

- In which situations is that perception accurate?
- Are there examples that refute that perception?

The answers to these two questions will enhance your understanding of who you are, what you value and where you're likely to enjoy your greatest success. You'll be more content with your choices and more confident in situations which previously spawned fear, anxiety and frustration.

Now that I know I'm doggedly aggressive when pursuing what I desire, less so with things that merely interest me, I've become more conscious and content with the decisions I make. I no longer ascribe the decision to hire people to clean my gutters or repair my roof to my fear of heights. I realize I could overcome that fear if I desired to do so. I overcame my fear of the water to become a scuba diver. Overcoming my fear of heights simply isn't that important to me.

As you become more aware of what's important to you, you'll make more conscious choices. While other people's perceptions can be valuable in this regard, don't accept them at face value. Realize that their perceptions are accurate in some situations and wholly inaccurate in others. This situational awareness helps you define what's important and what isn't. This knowledge leads to conscious decisions, greater contentment and greater confidence.

Surround yourself with people who believe in and encourage you. Use their perceptions of you to enhance your understanding of yourself and to apply what you learn in making conscious decisions. These are two of the three essential elements needed to maintain confidence during the pursuit of your dreams, including dark hours.

The third element is the methodology you use in setting goals. That's the topic of our next chapter.

CHAPTER 10
The cardinal rule of goals

It's October 2014 and the St. Louis Cardinals are in the playoffs for the fourth time in five years; the eleventh time in the past fifteen years. That's an impressive record. What's their secret?

I'm not enough of a fan to have a definitive answer to that question, assuming there is just one answer. What I am aware of is that the Cardinals' approach to goal setting is a key factor.

In an interview, former Cardinal's manager Tony La Russa, said that their goal was to win each series. He knew that if the team won enough series during the season, the Cardinals were assured a spot in the playoffs.

John Mozeliak, the Cardinal's general manager, offered a similar insight while recapping the Cardinal's 2014 season. He noted that, despite the team's struggles during the season, the Cardinals managed to achieve a winning record every month during the 2014 season.

La Russa's and Mozeliak's logic is so obvious that it's easy to overlook its power. Their message is simple—you will enjoy greater success when you establish interim goals. The psychological implication of this insight is huge.

Big (long-term) goals require months, possibly years, to achieve. Unless you can measure *and celebrate* success along the way, you're not likely to achieve your goal. The longer you have to wait for measurable progress, the more distant and less achievable your goal seems. Given the length of the baseball season, 162 games, it would be virtually impossible for players to stay focused on the goal of getting to the playoffs without interim goals.

The same is true for your long-term goals. Without interim goals you'll feel that you're expending significant amounts of time and energy with nothing to show for it. Consequently, your confidence as well as your desire to persevere wane. All too often this confluence of feelings results in you abandoning once-important goals and resigning yourself to a life of disappointment.

Interim goals enable you to enjoy a series of successes, which reinforce your belief that your goal is attainable. Success boosts your confidence and elevates your energy level. You feel successful because you are successful. As a result you'll dream bigger dreams and be confident in the knowledge that you can attain them.

Follow the cardinal rule of goals, establish interim goals, and celebrate success along the way to your long-term goal. You'll enjoy greater success, unshakable confidence and a life others desire.

The three elements for maintaining confidence while pursuing long-term goals are:

• Developing a support system of family and friends.
• Carefully analyzing other's perceptions of you.
• Setting interim goals.

These three elements dramatically improve the likelihood you'll survive the dark hours everyone experiences in pursuit of their long-term goals.

In this chapter we briefly touched upon perseverance. It's time to explore the role perseverance plays in building confidence.

CHAPTER 11
An overnight success?

Shortly after becoming famous Garth Brooks was asked, "How does it feel to be an overnight success?" His response was "Not bad considering it took fourteen years."

As I chuckled at his response, I recalled that the problem with success stories is that we rarely hear the whole story. Garth Brooks' response reminded us that he played a lot of smoke-filled bars, some with wire cages to protect the band, before he was "discovered."

Jack Canfield, co-author of the Chicken Soup book series, says that he received one hundred and forty-four (144) rejections before getting *Chicken Soup for the Soul* published.

The sharks, on the TV show *Shark Tank,* regularly cite failures they experienced as they explain to entrepreneurs why the business model they're proposing won't work or will be more challenging than the entrepreneur realizes.

Inspirational author and speaker, Og Mandino, reminds us of how important it is to tell the whole story. He relates an experience in which, after a presentation, a woman in the audience approached him. She said that his message was fine for people like him who had it all figured out, but that for the rest of the folks it wasn't helpful.

With that comment Mr. Mandino realized he needed to share his entire story—a story remarkable for the depth to which he'd fallen.

As I recall the story, he'd lost his job, his family, his home and was standing in front of a pawn shop eyeing a .38 revolver with $35 in his pocket.

For a reason that I doubt even he fully comprehended, he left the pawn shop window and went to the library where he began reading what he termed "the wisdom of the ages." The knowledge and inspiration he gained enabled him to climb out of that very deep hole and rise to a place where he enriched the lives of others.

My experiences mirror those cited above. It took over twenty years for me to transition from shy child to gregarious adult. The opportunity to start my own consulting business surfaced seventeen years after I first considered doing that work.

As I look back on these experiences, one of the things I realized is that, while I didn't have a formal plan for achieving these goals, I was always moving toward them.

Here's what I'd like you to take away from these stories:

1. Success is earned; it's never a gift.
2. Worthwhile endeavors require more time, energy and effort than you imagine.

"Overnight success" is a myth; one that needs to be dispelled. Anyone who achieves any measure of success, does so only after expending a great deal of effort. Acknowledge this fact and remind yourself of it often; it'll make it easier for you to persevere.

Now that you've discovered how to persevere, let's figure out what you need to do to recover from the inevitable mistakes you'll make. It's a lesson that's served me well.

CHAPTER 12
Recovery shots

Professional golfers are brutally honest with themselves. They *know* they're going to hit bad shots. Their success doesn't depend on whether they hit errant shots, but how quickly they can recover.

Pro golfers spend significant amounts of time practicing their recovery shots. They practice shots from sand traps, water's edge, under low-hanging limbs, behind trees and the rough (tall grass). One of the reasons they enjoy such great success, and possess such great confidence, is that they practice these recovery shots.

The most successful salespeople practice recovery. They know how quickly an innocuous statement, or poorly-crafted question, can cost them the sale. Instead of recovery shots, they have recovery scripts which they practice religiously. The language in these scripts rekindles the prospect's interest and salvages sales.

It's a practice that works well for me whether in a sales call or consulting session. Here's how it works.

Immediately following a sales call or consulting session, I replay the conversation in my mind. I recall the language that generated interest, excitement, and enabled us to move forward, then make a mental note to use this language again.

Next, I recall language that lost the person's interest or created confusion. I play with the language looking for ways to express my thoughts without losing the prospect's interest or creating confusion. Once I feel that I've achieved that goal, I make a mental note of that language.

This simple process has several advantages. It not only makes my language more precise; it limits the number of times I employ recovery scripts. The more precise I become in my language, the fewer problems I create for myself. The fewer problems I face, the greater my confidence. By the way, this approach works just as well in dealings with family and friends.

If you want to bolster your confidence, practice recovery shots. You'll discover that the more you practice, the less concern you have about making a mistake. You *know* that it's inevitable that you'll make mistakes, so why not prepare your recovery shots. It's a great way to minimize fear and anxiety.

Note that I said "minimize" fear and anxiety, not eliminate it. I also talk about being "virtually free" of fear, anxiety and frustration. There's a reason for the precision in that language —a reason you'll discover in chapter 13.

CHAPTER 13
Virtually free

Regardless of how confident you become or how successful you are, you'll never be completely free of fear, anxiety and frustration. Why? Because fear, anxiety and frustration are emotions. By definition, emotions are automatic responses. You can't *prevent* them. What you can do is control your reaction to them.

Despite the confidence I possess and good fortune I enjoy, there are times when I get frustrated because things aren't progressing the way I'd like. Opportunities trigger in me the same fears and anxiety you experience. No matter what we do, how confident we become, we never become immune to these emotions. The difference is that I've learned how to set these negative emotions aside more quickly than most people can.

The key is confidence. As I learned how to position myself to enjoy success in every endeavor my confidence grew, as did my ability to dismiss the negative emotions of fear, anxiety and frustration. I became aware of this fact through my dealings with clients.

After helping clients through what they perceived to be a dire situation, they would often ask me how I was able to remain so calm and craft such simple solutions while everyone else was frantic.

The answer is that I'm confident in my abilities to learn and adapt to any situation I face. Because my mind isn't burdened with fear, anxiety and frustration, it's free to focus on whatever challenge my client is facing. I'm able to listen more effectively, to be more objective and be open to a broader array of possible solutions, and remain calm in the face of adversity.

Another insight into the benefits of being virtually free of fear, anxiety and frustration, came from a friend who is a DISC behavioral profiler, upon viewing my profile, said "You have very little stress in your life." When I asked him why he said, "You've structured your life the way you want it to be." He was right on both counts.

As I stated earlier, I'm not immune to negative emotions. The confidence I've gained enables me to set them aside quickly and move forward. Sometimes that involves playing mind games on myself. Here's one of my less clever examples.

Without realizing it I'd become frustrated and despondent. Even though I knew I was doing all the right things, I wasn't getting the results I desired.

This went on until I realized that I wasn't putting forth the effort needed to achieve my goal. As soon as I became aware of this fact I thought "Okay, Dale, you've got one hour for a pity party, then you have to get back to work."

I sat back in my chair, propped my feet on the desk, prepared to feel sorry for myself for an hour. After forty-five seconds I thought, "This is the dumbest thing I've ever done." I began laughing and immediately went back to work, fully energized and optimistic that I would succeed, which I did.

Ever since that episode, whenever I feel afraid, anxious or frustrated, I mentally tell myself that I've got an hour for a pity party. I begin laughing and go right back to work.

I may not be able to eliminate negative emotions, but I can dismiss them in a few seconds with a single thought.

That's my wish for you—that you're able to, within a few seconds, set aside any negative emotions you're feeling. When you are able to do that, you'll lead a life virtually free of fear, anxiety and frustration—a life others desire.

The fact that emotions are automatic responses that can't be prevented but can be displaced begs the question: "What roles do your subconscious and conscious minds play in developing confidence?" That's the topic of our next chapter.

CHAPTER 14
Conscious vs. subconscious?

In our discussion of "virtually free," we got a glimpse into the workings of our conscious and subconscious minds. To get a more thorough understanding let's explore an experience I'm certain each of you has had.

A problem surfaces; you spend the entire day seeking a solution to no avail. The next morning, during your shower, the solution pops into your mind. The answer is so obvious that you wonder "Why didn't I think of that before?"

The answer to that question lies in understanding the roles of your conscious and subconscious minds—an understanding I gained after reading Dr. Joseph Murphy's book, *The Power of Your Subconscious Mind*.

Your subconscious mind is a processor; it's functions are managing vital bodily functions and processing data you feed it. This processor function is what enables the subconscious mind to solve problems that baffle the conscious mind.

The conscious mind controls input into your subconscious mind. Your interaction with your computer emulates the way your subconscious and conscious minds work together. You control input into your computer, the computer processes that input. Now that we have a sense of each mind's roles, let's see what implications that has for dealing with emotions.

48

Your subconscious mind processes the information you feed it. If you're experiencing fear, anxiety, or frustration *and* dwell on these feelings, you're feeding these emotions into your subconscious mind.

Like your computer your subconscious has no choice; it must accept that input. If you want a different result, you must change the input. In other words, you have to make a conscious choice to set aside the emotions that are preventing you from achieving your goal. Here's an example to illustrate this point.

My wife and I were planning a trip to the Caribbean when she said "I'd like to see the fish in their natural habitat."

"Fine, we can go snorkeling."

She said "I want to scuba dive."

I've always been a lousy swimmer. I also feared the water. Scuba diving was not an aspiration. At the same time I didn't want to deprive my wife of an experience she desired. I knew I'd have to overcome my fear to make her dream come true.

Given that input my subconscious noted that while I wasn't a strong swimmer, I could manage the distance required to qualify for the course. After each lesson I'd wonder what I could do to become more comfortable performing that exercise. My subconscious repeatedly found ways for me to overcome whatever fear I was experiencing.

It's been over thirty years since my wife and I became certified divers. We have had the good fortune to enjoy scuba diving around the world and look forward to more diving in the future.

It's worth noting that the reason I was able to overcome my fear was that I *desired* to share my wife's scuba experiences. Absent that desire, I would not have expended the time and energy it took to overcome my fear of the water.

The second element of my success in overcoming my fear of the water was the conscious choice I made to overcome that fear. Once I made that choice, my subconscious mind found ways for me to become comfortable scuba diving. To this day, I'm more comfortable diving than I am swimming. That's the power your subconscious mind possesses.

Dr. Murphy suggests that we will achieve a great deal more as we become more adept at engaging our subconscious minds. He counsels that, when faced with a confounding problem, instead of trying to force a conscious solution, turn the problem over to your subconscious and shift your focus to something you can accomplish. You'll avoid stress and enjoy greater success.

His advice made it easier for me to overcome my fear of the water. Instead of consciously trying to find ways to become more comfortable, I'd wonder what would make diving more comfortable. Then I'd do something else.

In essence, I turned the problem over to my subconscious mind and allowed it to find the solution for me. It worked precisely the way Dr. Murphy said it would.

Whenever you find yourself experiencing fear, anxiety or frustration, make a conscious choice not to dwell on these emotions. Instead, ask your subconscious what you need to do to become successful, then shift your focus onto something you can accomplish.

This simple technique will help you be more productive, solve problems more quickly, enjoy more energy and greater confidence. That's a lot of benefit from one action.

Thanks, Dr. Murphy.

The next challenge to our confidence we're going to tackle is the dichotomy between contentment and desire. Is it possible to be both content and desirous at the same time? Let's find out.

CHAPTER 15
Contentment vs. desire?

My wife and I were visiting a recently-opened store when we spotted a Thomas Kinkade tapestry. Despite its beauty, what caught my eye was the Joseph Addison quote that appeared at the bottom. Addison said "A contented mind is the greatest blessing a man can enjoy in this world."

That tapestry hangs just inside our bedroom door. It's one of the first things I see each day. That quote reminds me to enjoy my life while pursuing unfulfilled dreams.

Contentment and desire are often viewed as conflicting emotions. How can we be content if we want more? What we fail to realize is that contentment and desire are both sources of great joy.

Contentment

When you're content with your life, warts and all, you experience joy that transcends whatever challenges you face. The key is knowing contentment is a choice.

While you already know that, it's easy to forget when you face problems, disappointment, fear and anxiety. That's why it's essential that you take a few moments each day to remind yourself of the good that exists in your life—loved ones, the success you've enjoyed, the kindness of strangers, things that make you smile—for it's in these memories that you find contentment.

The Addison quote reminds me that I can be content despite the challenges I face. I understand that difficulties are merely stepping stones to higher levels of contentment. As you discover contentment, you too will enjoy greater confidence and a more optimistic attitude.

Just as importantly, you'll discover that contentment doesn't inhibit desire, it intensifies it.

Desire

As you remind yourself of all the good that exists in your life, you spark a desire for more—as it should. The pursuit of greater joy and contentment gives our lives purpose.

It's an often-overlooked fact that there is greater joy in pursuit than in achievement. You don't have to take my word for it, simply recall a goal you achieved. How long were you satisfied with that achievement? A day? A week? A month or two?

Whatever the time frame, the joy of accomplishment is fleeting. Every achievement leaves us wanting more. That's okay because within desire lies purpose—within purpose, a happier, healthier life. Again you don't have to trust me, a study by Harvard psychologist Ellen Langer substantiates this claim.

Dr. Langer's researchers provided plants to two hundred residents in a nursing facility. One hundred residents were told that the facility would care for the plants. The other group was responsible for the plant's care.

The results are fascinating. Residents responsible for the plant's care enjoyed a lower mortality rate. Less than half of them had died compared to those whose plants were cared for by the facility. Being responsible for the care of a living organism gave the second group enough purpose to enable them to enjoy greater health and longevity.

Advancing the welfare of others gives us purpose and a sense of value. Emerson said "It is one of the most beautiful compensations in life...that no man can sincerely try to help another without helping himself."

Our desire to become better spouses, parents, friends, more productive, more knowledgeable, more valuable to society brings us immeasurable joy while enriching the lives of others.

When desire is absent, we become complacent. We waste our talents and deprive ourselves and others of the joy we could have created. We no longer live; we merely exist.

Don't let anyone tell you that you can't be content *and* desirous simultaneously. These emotions aren't just congruent, they're complementary; contentment sparks greater, more intense desire, which enables you to achieve more and, in doing so, enrich your life as well as the lives of others. It's how you create a life others desire.

The good news is that you get to choose whether you want a life rich in contentment and desire or one plagued by fear, anxiety and frustration. Choose wisely.

As you accomplish more, your confidence grows. In the next chapter we'll explore techniques for accelerating that growth.

CHAPTER 16
Accelerating growth

It was a dreary, cold, rainy Saturday; ideal for nestling in with a hot chocolate and good book. Unfortunately, I had just finished the book I'd been reading. When I got to the library, I realized that my usual mystery/thriller fare didn't hold much appeal.

As I browsed the stacks looking for an intriguing title, my eyes fell upon a book entitled *Playing Ball on Running Water*— a treasure much greater than I could have imagined.

The author, David Reynolds, is a psychotherapist who studied both in the United States and in Japan. In *Playing Ball*, he noted that the primary difference between eastern and western approaches to psychotherapy is that western therapists spend a lot of time trying to ascertain *why* people behave the way they do while eastern therapists could care less. Eastern therapists focus on helping patients develop more productive behaviors.

I found this observation comforting. My experience had been that whenever I ascribed motivations to my clients' behaviors, I was usually wrong. Using the eastern approach I not only avoided these mistakes, I helped clients develop behaviors that produced great results quickly.

If you want to accelerate the growth in your confidence, stop trying to figure out why you're doing what you're doing. Instead, identify behaviors that will produce the results you want, then invest your time in making those behaviors a habit.

One of the questions I'm often asked is "How will I know that my confidence is growing?" The answer lies in the frequency with which you express confidence—chapter 17's topic.

CHAPTER 17
Expressing confidence

In a matter of seconds you can tell how confident a person is. If I asked you how you know, odds are you'd struggle to come up with an answer. Why?

We sense confidence more than comprehend it—just as we sense an oncoming storm before any signs appear. Let's explore behaviors that enable us to sense a person's confidence.

The confident people I know are calm, candid and caring. Each of these behaviors expresses confidence that other people sense and, more importantly, tap into to help them overcome the obstacles they face. Exploring each of these behaviors in greater detail will help you become aware of the confidence you're expressing.

Calm

During the seventh game of the 2014 World Series, Giant's ace Madison Bumgarner, on two days' rest, takes the field in the fifth inning and pitches five scoreless innings to seal the Giants win over Kansas City.

When Bumgarner was in the dugout, the cameras would zoom in and find him amazingly calm, yet intensely focused. He appeared to be in a zen-like state. That's the look and feel of confidence.

Professional football players describe this feeling by saying that the game "slows down." In other words, they see what's going on so clearly, it's as if the game is being played in slow motion. Imagine how much more productive you'll be, how effective your listening skills will be, and how much easier it will be to find solutions to the challenges you face, when the game slows down.

"Zen-like state" and "slowing the game down" are vivid descriptions of the feelings you'll experience as your confidence grows.

The following exchange is typical of what I've experienced over the years in working with clients. It highlights the way others will perceive your calm demeanor and the impact it has upon them.

> *"How do you do it?"*
> *"Do what?"*
> *"Remain so calm. It doesn't matter how dire the situation seems or how frantic those around you are, you remain calm and craft a simple solution to the problem."*

The simple answer is that confidence slows the game down for me just as it does for professional football players. I see things more clearly and hear things others miss because they're frantic. Because I possess a mind that's free of fear, anxiety and frustration, I'm able to see alternatives others overlook. I'm also able to evaluate a broad array of options to discern which is the simplest, least expensive and easiest to implement.

Confidence, and the calm it engenders, come from things we've already discussed:

- The definition of success.
- The ability to learn.
- Practicing recovery shots.
- Competing only with yourself.
- Effectively using your subconscious mind.
- Being content.

Remaining calm affords you a number of advantages. Here are examples to illustrate that point.

Emergency medical people know that the likelihood of making a mistake drops dramatically when they remain calm. In their line of work, mistakes can be fatal. That's why, other than on TV, you don't see EMTs racing to the injured party.

Instead, they take time to assure they'll have the equipment and supplies they'll need *before* approaching the victim. Their deliberate actions assure calm and focus, which increases the likelihood of the patient's survival. With minds free of fear, anxiety and frustration, they're better able to assess the situation accurately and employ the most effective treatments for their patients' survival. They know that the cool head prevails. I learned this lesson while providing part-time CFO services for a client.

The client's principals called me into their office and railed at me, non-stop, for forty-five minutes. Their complaint? They weren't getting information they needed to make good decisions—to manage effectively.

Confidence enabled me to remain quiet while they were venting their frustration. At the end of their rant, I paused to make sure that they were finished. Then I quietly, calmly said "You're right. You should be getting that information. But, if you recall, I've been telling you that neither the computer system nor the staff is adequate to handle the volume you're adding."

They looked at one another, then asked "What do we need to do, Dale?" I told them what we needed and got everything I requested. The cool head prevailed.

As you become more confident, you'll become calm. The game will slow down, you'll see things more clearly and your mind will be free of fear and anxiety. You *know* that you'll be successful.

You also know that while missteps and set backs are inevitable, they can't deprive you of what you truly desire. It's not a question of *if*, but *when* you'll be successful.

Like Garth Brooks, you're aware that achieving your goal will take time and, like the Cardinals, you've positioned yourself to enjoy interim success.

As you become more confident, you'll be attributed with "quiet confidence." One way to gauge your progress is the frequency with which others describe you this way.

Confident people are also candid. That's the second of our three confident behaviors and our next topic.

Candid

First and foremost confident people are candid with themselves. They are honest with themselves about what they do well and when they need help. Confident people don't put a spin on their mistakes; everyone makes mistakes. They also know others will forgive their mistakes as long as their intent is good.

As you become more confident you'll become more candid with yourself. You'll also find that you're able to be candid with others without being critical or denigrating. In the CFO example, I was candid with the principals without attacking their earlier decisions or denigrating them. My statement was factual and devoid of criticism. These we're essential elements in getting what I needed.

Confident people don't embrace the adage that the best defense is a good offense. They don't attack others to protect themselves. Instead, they elevate others so that they too can enjoy greater success and confidence, which leads to our third confident behavior—caring.

Caring

With confidence, you transcend the boundaries of contentment to live a life of joy. One of the fascinating aspects of joy is that you want to share it. Recall any good news you received—a promotion, unexpected praise, a kindness you didn't expect—you couldn't wait to share the good news. Confident people can't wait to share their confidence and joy with others.

A caring attitude manifests itself in a couple of ways. Confident people, regardless of how hectic their schedule is, take time to help others. They put the needs of others ahead of their own because they *know* that their needs, their goals, their aspirations will be met.

They *know* that they have the power to persevere when things aren't going as well as expected, to remain focused and optimistic in the face of disappointment, to recover from missteps and, using the definition of success, be successful in every endeavor. Given this mindset why wouldn't they take time to help others.

Caring also manifests itself in the form of encouragement. The Williams sisters were surrounded by naysayers. They had to develop new friendships to gain the encouragement they knew was essential to achieving their dreams. You may have to as well; we all need encouragement from time to time.

It's possible that, in the past, you were a naysayer. No more. As you gain confidence, you'll transition from naysayer to encourager. You'll want others to experience the joy you've discovered. As you share your joy you'll become known as a confident, caring person.

Now that you know how confidence manifests itself and how to use that knowledge to evaluate your progress in gaining confidence, let's see what it's like to live with confidence.

CHAPTER 18
Living with confidence

What's it like to live confidently? Think of the confident people you know. What do you notice about them? Closing your eyes may help you see them more clearly.

You probably noticed that they're always sporting a big smile. They're content with who they are and the lives they've created.

They're calm even when things don't seem to be going their way. They don't seem to be afraid of anything; indeed they seem to welcome challenges that test them. Challenges most people would find devastating are mere inconveniences to them. In other words, their lives seem easy.

Their lives are easy *now*, but that wasn't always the case. All confident people go through a process of discovery during which they learn what it takes to be confident. Then they work diligently to develop their confidence. While some may have had a head start in that they're "wired" with greater confidence than you or I, none of them achieved contentment without considerable effort.

Now that we have a sense for what it's like to live confidently, let's review some of the elements needed for growing confidence. The first element is desire.

Desire

At the heart of any accomplishment, great or small, is desire. Without desire there is no effort; without effort, no achievement. It's a basic human tenet that your personal history will verify.

You've seen proof from my personal history. My desire for the company of others sustained me during the nearly twenty years it took to overcome my fear of meeting new people. I wanted my wife to enjoy the experience of scuba diving. That desire enabled me to persevere during the months it took to overcome my fear of the water. Conversely, I don't have a desire to climb mountains, skydive, bungee jump, or walk a tightrope so I'm not going to invest time, effort or energy into overcoming my fear of heights. Your personal history is replete with similar examples.

The question that only you can answer is "How important is it to *you* that you live confidently—that you enjoy the benefits confident people enjoy?" The fact that you've read this far into the book is a pretty good indicator that you have a *strong* desire to become more confident, to be more content, to live virtually free of fear, anxiety and frustration. Desire exists; let's see what's needed to persevere.

Expectations
Fear and anxiety

Fear and anxiety are the progeny of expectation. Recall a time when you were afraid or at least anxious. I'm not a betting man, but I'll bet it was a situation in which you had little if any familiarity. In other words, you didn't know what to expect.

Regardless of whether you received a job offer, earned a promotion, encountered health issues, learned that you were becoming a parent, you faced uncertainty. That uncertainty triggered feelings of doubt, fear and anxiety even when the news was good. Here are some fears and doubts we all experience in good news situations.

With a new job, you wonder: "Will I like my new job? Can I be successful? Will I like my boss? Am I making a mistake?"

A promotion triggers different concerns. You wonder: "Will my staff follow my lead? Will I have the answers to their questions, the solutions to their problems? What do I do when an employee fails to meet expectations—fails to perform?"

When expecting your first child you wonder "Will I be a good parent? Will he or she be healthy? Will I be able to cope with the problems that will inevitably arise? Am I ready to be responsible for another human being's welfare? Can I keep my child safe? Am I making enough money to support a child?"

With health issues our minds immediately go to the worst case scenario. Indeed, in all uncertain situations we're wired to expect the worst possible outcome. It's one of the less desirable aspects of our human nature. We'll talk about how you can overcome these natural tendencies in a moment. Before we do let's explore the link between frustration and expectation.

Frustration

When we compare fear and anxiety with frustration, we see that the primary difference is their origin. Fear and anxiety are borne of uncertainty; frustration is the progeny of unreasonable expectations.

The Garth Brooks' interview offers an excellent example of how easily unreasonable expectations are created. During the interview, Mr. Brooks was asked what it felt like to be an overnight success. This question fosters the unreasonable expectation that instantaneous success is possible. Nothing could be further from the truth.

As we saw in earlier examples, anyone who achieves anything worthwhile does so through hard work and perseverance. Here are more examples to illustrate this point.

Pro golfer Jack Nicklaus was reportedly seen driving golf balls into the wind during a driving rain storm. It's been said that Phil Mickelson doesn't quit practice sessions until he sinks one hundred consecutive puts. That's the effort required to enjoy great success; it doesn't happen overnight.

The overnight success myth isn't the only mistaken belief under which many of us labor. We believe that talent assures success, superior products win the marketplace, that successful people are blessed in a special way, that other people's lives are easier than our own. We deceive ourselves when we embrace these myths.

The late Og Mandino described it this way: "Nothing is so easy as to deceive one's self since what we wish is always easy to believe. No one, in my life, has deceived me as much as I have."

If you're experiencing frustration, it's because you're deceiving yourself—you're expecting success without desire, hard work or the perseverance it requires.

Once you identify which of these elements is missing, make a conscious decision about how important the goal is to you. If it's important enough for you to change your behavior, to do what you need to do to be successful, then continue pursuing your goal. If it's not important, consciously shift your focus to something that you are passionate enough about to be successful.

Conscious choices have the power to eliminate frustration. They force you to examine how important your goal is to you, what it'll take to achieve your goal and whether you're willing to commit the time, energy and effort required to be successful.

Good news

You have the power to set reasonable expectations and overcome the natural tendencies that create fear, anxiety and frustration. To minimize frustration, establish reasonable expectations. You *know* things aren't going to go according to plan. Expect it; it's inevitable. Expect it to take longer to achieve your goal than you anticipate, it almost always does.

One of the ways to become more realistic in your expectations is to examine prior successes. Embedded in these successes is your history of overcoming obstacles, persevering in the face of adversity, growing stronger and more confident as you move closer and closer to your goal. As you reflect on earlier successes, the challenges you overcame and the time it took to achieve them, your expectations become more realistic.

When you expect problems you equip yourself emotionally and mentally to deal with those difficulties. In those rare instances when things go better than expected, you can enjoy them without deluding yourself into believing that somehow life is going to get easier.

Recalling earlier successes is a great way to deal with fear and anxiety as well as frustration. The difference lies in the takeaway. With frustration your review of earlier successes uncovers unrealistic expectations. For fear and anxiety, your review reminds you that it isn't knowledge or experience that matter, it's your ability to learn and adapt.

During your review you'll recall the jobs you've had, how little you knew going in, and the success you enjoyed despite a lack of experience. Recalling earlier successes makes it easier to set aside the fear and anxiety new opportunities typically spawn.

Another technique for alleviating fear and anxiety is recalling how rarely your worst fears are realized. It's natural for our minds to imagine the worst case scenario, but these thoughts persist only when we nurture them. You can replace fears and anxiety with a more optimistic outlook by remembering how seldom your fears are realized. Remember that your subconscious mind can be a powerful ally in shifting your thinking.

It's also helpful to remember the good that came out of previous adversity. Nothing that you experience is all good or all bad. If you look for the good that may come from the challenge you're facing, you'll find it and be less fearful. As you'll recall from our definition of success, if things don't work out but you learned something it's still a success.

Finally, remember that the future is *always* uncertain. You live with uncertainty everyday, from the moment you get up until you awaken the next morning. If you're already facing uncertainty, why forgo an opportunity that intrigues you simply because the outcome is uncertain?

By reviewing prior successes, you become more realistic in your expectations and replace worst-case scenarios with positive results. With each review fear, anxiety and frustration abate, enabling you to become more aware of your surroundings—another great benefit.

Aware

When your mind isn't busy nurturing fear, anxiety or frustration, it's free to see things others don't see, to craft solutions others never imagined, to encourage others during their darkest hours.

This level of awareness will have others saying "You don't think like other people do. You see the world differently than other people do. You see things others don't see." They're right. You'll possess an ability few possess.

To fully understand how powerful these impressions are, it's helpful to reverse roles and make you the recipient of someone else's wisdom. Here's an experience I'm certain you've had.

You've been fretting for days over a problem you're facing. You run into a friend and share your concerns with her. Within seconds, she offers an insight that leaves you wondering "Why didn't I think of that?" At that moment you think your friend is brilliant.

The reality is that your friend isn't any brighter than you are, but she has an advantage—her mind isn't plagued by the fear, anxiety and frustration you're experiencing.

The more adept you become at setting these emotions aside, the more quickly you'll find solutions to whatever problems you face. Over time you'll become so adept and your awareness so heightened that you'll spend less time solving problems because you're adept at avoiding them. Your consistent practice of recovery shots helps you anticipate problems and develop preemptive strategies to prevent them from occurring.

The freedom your mind experiences also enables you to become more deliberate in making decisions.

Deliberate

Most people's choices are driven by emotion. That's as true for positive emotions like hope and desire as it is for fear, anxiety and frustration.

When I first saw the Samsung ad where two people transferred files by touching their Galaxy phones together, my reaction was "I gotta have that." Then I realized that I only use my iPhone to make calls and check my calendar. Because I'd never use that feature, I made a conscious (deliberate) choice not to purchase one. I avoided wasting money on something I'd never use.

That's just one example of the benefits you gain from making deliberate choices—as confidence grows you diminish the impact emotions have on your decision-making process. You become more deliberate in making decisions. The more deliberate your decisions, the more well aligned they are with what you truly desire. Here's a personal story to give you a sense for what alignment can do for you.

I was invited to complete a DISC profile questionnaire which I did. The resulting report included a page of concentric circles with two symbols superimposed on these circles.

The first symbol represented my natural style, the second my adaptive style (an indication of the degree to which I had adapted to my environment). On an 8.5" x 11" sheet of paper, a quarter of an inch separated the two symbols.

When I asked the DISC practitioner what those symbols indicated, he said "You have very little stress in your life." I agreed and asked "Why do you say that?" He responded "You have structured your life the way you want it to be." He was right on both counts.

That's the life I want for you. I want you to be able to make deliberate choices, to structure your life the way you want it to be, to be content while continuously striving for more.

Wait, there's more. You'll also discover that you enjoy greater influence as you become more confident.

Influential

Confidence stimulates trust. You know that's true. You're likely to believe a confident person and distrust a person that's waffling. You'll also recall that you're less likely to refute what a confident person is saying.

There are a number of reasons why we trust confident people. First and foremost they're honest; in particular, they're honest with themselves. They don't try to look smarter than they are, they don't hide their mistakes, or put a spin on them so they don't look quite as stupid as they are in that moment. Instead, most of them laugh at their mistakes. These are the reasons why we trust confident people.

Couple that honesty with their heightened awareness—their ability to see things you don't see as well as their ability to craft simple, inexpensive, easy-to-implement solutions for the problems you face—not only do you trust them, you seek their advice. Who wouldn't turn to someone possessing these formidable skills?

As your confidence grows, you'll become that person. The more frequently others seek your assistance, the more influence you gain. As your influence grows, so does your ability to enrich the lives of others. The more people you help, the more valuable you become.

Over the years a few people have expressed concern that they'd be tempted to abuse this power—to use it for personal gain at the expense of others. While it's possible, it's highly unlikely.

First, the fact that you are concerned means that you'll monitor your behavior to prevent it from happening. Second, confident people experience such great joy that they want to share it. It's an unselfish joy—one that acknowledges that joy is limitless regardless of how often it's shared. A passage from the *Isavasya Upanishad* expresses it this way:

> *"That is full; this is full;*
> *Fullness comes forth from fullness:*
> *When fullness is taken from fullness,*
> *Fullness remains."*

In other words joy is limitless, which brings us to the ultimate benefit confidence affords, joyful living.

Joyful

As your confidence grows, so does your joy of living. You're virtually free of fear, anxiety and frustration. You are making deliberate choices about what you want out of life. Your investing the time, energy and effort needed to make your dreams come true.

You have reasonable expectations. You know that you'll make mistakes along the way. But you're practicing your recovery shots so that any mistakes you make are temporary setbacks.

Heightened awareness enables you to see what others don't see and craft solutions others can't imagine. In doing so you enrich the lives of others, while gaining tremendous influence.

Armed with a new definition of success, you *know* that you're going to be successful in every endeavor *regardless of the outcome.* You understand that getting a "No" saves you time and energy, that disappointing results are an investment in a brighter future *as long as you learned something.* You appreciate these lessons even when you don't get the result you were seeking.

The joy you experience is a by-product of being confident —of being virtually free of fear, anxiety and frustration. Your joy will be so obvious that you'll have people telling you "I want your life!" That's my wish for you—a life so rich in joy that others desire it.

— *Dale Furtwengler*

DAILY CONFIDENCE BUILDER

Contentment
Both desire and contentment are sources of great joy. Pursue your dreams aggressively while enjoying the good that already exists in your life.

Expectations
Realize that achieving your goal will take more time, effort and energy than you imagine. Remember that the joy of achievement is fleeting, the joy of pursuit endless.

Interim success
Each day take a few minutes to review your successes, including the times you gave someone a reason to smile or encouraged them during a dark period.

Virtually free
Remember that emotions are automatic responses. While you can't avoid them, you can control your response to them. One of the quickest, most effective ways to free yourself of fear, anxiety and frustration is to recall prior successes.

Problems
Don't waste time trying to solve perplexing problems, turn them over to your subconscious mind, then shift your efforts to something you can accomplish consciously.

Recovery shots
Practice your recovery shots every day. The more you practice, the more likely you are to preclude the need for them.

74

EXCERPT FROM

Introduction

Congratulations! You've taken the critical first step to becoming invaluable – you've decided to take action.

Your decision to employ the 7 Steps demonstrates that you have the desire, passion and determination to create a better life for yourself—a life that is simultaneously easier and more productive. How can this be? The 7 Steps to Becoming INVALUABLE shows you how to minimize the challenges our human nature creates for us.

By virtue of our humanity, we:

1. naturally want to protect our ego and blame others when things aren't going well
2. try to persuade others when that isn't possible
3. judge others and the situations we face as being good or bad
4. fail to see similarities in seemingly diverse situations
5. participate in group think when the voice of reason tells us not to
6. specialize so narrowly that we limit our potential
7. have a difficult time knowing which opportunities are right for us

I'd love to tell you that I'm exempt from these challenges, but I possess the same human nature you do. Just like you, I cannot eliminate these aspects of my humanity. I have, however, learned how to minimize their impact so dramatically that living has become easy. Even during the most challenging times, I'm able to set my emotions aside and deal with the issues as they are, not as I'd like them to be. In doing so, I:

- minimize the fear and anxiety these situations would normally create
- identify potential solutions more quickly than ever before
- act with confidence because of the clarity counter-intuitive thinking affords
- enjoy better results more quickly, further diminishing the periods of anxiety

In addition to minimizing the emotional roller coaster human nature has set for us, I've attracted opportunities that I'd never dreamed—opportunities to write books for major publishing houses, to share what I've learned with audiences and in self-study courses like this one. Each of these opportunities provides both psychic and financial rewards beyond my wildest dreams. In fact, my good fortune has me looking at the world as a big playground and I haven't played with all the toys yet.

That's my wish for you – that through the 7 Steps to Becoming INVALUABLE you'll find a world filled with toys you haven't imagined and you get to pick and choose which ones you want to play with. If you find that you don't enjoy a toy you've chosen, no problem! There are always more waiting for you. Let's find that playground!

— *Dale Furtwengler*

About the author

Dale Furtwengler is a coach, professional speaker and internationally-acclaimed author who helps his clients enjoy greater personal, professional, and business success.

Each of Dale's books provide insights into behaviors that drive, or deprive, people of the success they desire. These behaviors are identified by observing incongruities between what people say and what they do. It's in these incongruities that the secrets to leading a life virtually free of fear, anxiety and frustration lie.

A former CFO, Dale has been a guest speaker at Webster and Lindenwood Universities and Fontbonne College. He also co-hosted Lindenwood University's Business Roundtable TV program. Bisk Education Services interviewed Dale on several occasions for their continuing education series for CPAs and he's been quoted in the *Harvard Management Communication Letter*.

In addition to *Lead a Life of Confidence,* Dale is the author of *Become a Maverick*, *Pricing for Profit*, *The 10-Minute Guide to Performance Appraisals*, *The Uniqueness Myth...and other misconceptions that derail businesses*, *Making the Exceptional Normal*, and *7 Steps to Becoming Invaluable*.

Dale's blogs appear on a variety of sites, including BestThinking.com and RetailCustomerExperience.com. Dale is an adjunct faculty member at the University of Missouri–St. Louis and lives in St. Louis, MO.

For more information on how you can increase your confidence, awareness, and gain a life free of fear, anxiety and frustration, visit: http://TheLifeOthersDesire.com.